100% The Vampire Diaries: The Unofficial Guide To The Vampire Diaries

A BANTAM BOOK 978 0 857 51037 2
First published in Great Britain by Bantam,
an imprint of Random House Children's Books
A Random House Group Company
Bantam edition published 2010
1 3 5 7 9 10 8 6 4 2
Text copyright © Bantam Books, 2010
Design by Shubrook Bros. Creative
www.shubrookbros.com

With special thanks to Louise Grosart, Ruth Knowles, Natalie Barnes, Ellie Farmer, Tamsan Barratt and Sharon Gosling

Cover photos © Ken McKay/Rex Features

Interior photos: Pg2 and Pg62(TL) © MCP/Rex Features, (TR) © Getty Images, (ML) © Startraks Photo/Rex Features, (B) © Getty Images. Pg3 and Pg63(all) © Getty Images, Pg 6-7 (all) © Getty Images (for inserts see relevant pages) & (BG)© istock, Pg 8 (T) © Getty Images, (BL) © Alex Segre/Rex Features, (BG) © Corey Hochachka / Design Pics Inc./Rex Features, Pg9 (L) © Getty Images, (M) ©MCP/Rex Features, (R) © Everett Collection/Rex Features, Pg 10 (L) © MCP/Rex Features, (BG) © Getty Images, (BG) © David Chapman / Design Pics Inc./Rex Features, Pg 11 (BG) © David Chapman / Design Pics Inc./Rex Features, (main) © Getty Images, (R) ©Michael Snell / Robert Harding/Rex Features, Pg 12-13 All © Getty Images, Pg 14 (BG) © Getty Images, (main) © Getty Images, (R) © Sipa Press/Rex Features, Pg 15 (BG) © Getty Images, (R) © Matt Baron/BEI/Rex Features, P16 (TL,TR) © Getty Images, (bottom images L-R) © MCP/Rex Features, ©Getty Images, © Hugh Thompson/Rex Features, © Startraks Photo/Rex Features, Pg17 (TL) ©Sipa Press/Rex Features, (TM) © Startraks Photo/Rex Features, (TR) ©Getty Images, (MM) ©Getty Images, (ML) ©Peter Brooker/Rex Features, (MR) © Getty Images, (BL) ©Peter Brooker/Rex Features, (BM) © Getty Images, Pg18-19 All © Getty Images, Pg20 (BG) © Getty Images, (M) © Startraks Photo/Rex Features, Pg21 (BG) © Getty Images, (L) © Startraks Photo/Rex Features, (R) © MCP/Rex Features, Pg22 (BG & M) © Getty Images, Pg23 (BG) © Getty Images, (L) © Sipa Press/Rex Features, (R) © Getty Images (BR) Startraks Photo/Rex Features, Pg24-25 All © Getty Images, Pg26 All © Getty Images except (MM) MCP/Rex Features and (BM) © Sipa Press/Rex Features, Pg27 (ML) © Peter Brooker/Rex Features, (BL) © Startraks Photo/Rex Features, (MM) ©Getty Images, (BM) © Getty Images, (MR) © Peter Brooker/Rex Features, (BR) © Startraks Photo/Rex Features, Pg 28 (BG) ©RITOLA/Rex Features, (main) © Getty Images, Pg29 (T) ©Getty Images, (B) © Rex Features, Pg30 (BG) ©Rex Features, (main) ©Hugh Thompson/Rex Features, Pg31 (BG) ©RITOLA/Rex Features, (B) © Getty Images, Pg32 (BG) © Getty Images, (BG-M) ©RITOLA/Rex Features, (main)© Startraks Photo/Rex Features, Pg33 All ©Getty Images, Pg34 (BG) © Getty Images, (BG) © istock, (main) © MCP/Rex Features, Pg35 (main) © Getty Images, Pg36 (BG) © Natural Selection Robert Cable / Design Pics Inc./Rex Features, (BG of pic frame) © Nicholas Bailey/Rex Features, (main) ©Peter Brooker/Rex Features, Pg37 (BG) ©Action Press/Rex Features, (main) © Sipa Press/Rex Features, Pg38-39 All © Getty Images, Pg40 All © Getty Images, Pg41 (main) © Getty Images, (BG) © istock, Pg42 (BG) ©David Chapman / Design Pics Inc./Rex Features, (main) © Getty Images, Pg43 (BG) © RITOLA/Rex Features, (main) ©Getty Images, Pg44-45 All © Getty Images, Pg46-47 All © Getty Images except (b/g) © istock, Pg48 (BG) © Natural Selection Robert Cable / Design Pics Inc./Rex Features, (main) © Getty Images, Pg49 (BG) © RITOLA/Rex Features, (main) © Startraks Photo/Rex Features, Pg50 (BG) ©Getty Images, (main) © Peter Brooker/Rex Features, Pg51 All © Getty Images, Pg52 (TL) © Getty Images, (TM) © Sipa Press/Rex Features, (TR) © Jim Smeal/BEI/Rex Features, (M) © Sipa Press/Rex Features, (B) © Getty Images, Pg53 © Getty Images, Pg54-55 All © Getty Images, Pg56 (main) © Everett Collection/Rex Features, (BL) © Startraks Photo/Rex Features, Pg57 (T) © Startraks Photo/Rex Features, (B) © Sipa Press/Rex Features, Pg58 (TL) ©Sipa Press/Rex Features, (TR) © Getty Images, (B) ©Startraks Photo/Rex Features, Pg59 (T) © Getty Images x2, (BL) © Matt Baron/BEI/Rex Features, (BR) © Startraks Photo/Rex Features., Pg60-61 ©Jim Smeal/BEI/Rex Features, (BG) ©KPA/Zuma/Rex Features, Pg62 (TL) © MCP/Rex Features, (TR) © Getty Images, (ML) © Startraks Photo/Rex Features, (B) © Getty Images.

All rights reserved. No part of this publication may be reproduced, stored in a retrieval system, or transmitted in any form or by any means, electronic, mechanical, photocopying, recording or otherwise, without the prior permission of the publishers.

Bantam Books are published by
Random House Children's Books,
61–63 Uxbridge Road, London W5 5SA
www.rbooks.co.uk

www.kidsatrandomhouse.co.uk

Addresses for companies within The Random House Group Limited can be found at:
www.randomhouse.co.uk/offices.htm

THE RANDOM HOUSE GROUP Limited Reg. No. 954009
A CIP catalogue record for this book is available from the British Library
Printed and bound by Scotprint, Haddington

THE UNOFFICIAL GUIDE TO THE VAMPIRE DIARIES

100% The Vampire Diaries

BANTAM BOOKS

EVIE PARKER

Contents

PAGE 9

THE CHARACTERS

Stefan Salvatore 10
Damon Salvatore 12
Elena Gilbert............................... 14
Love Bites 16
Bonnie Bennett,
Caroline Forbes &
Matt Donovan 20
Vicki Donovan,
Jeremy Gilbert,
Tyler Lockwood & Anna............ 22
Alaric Saltzman,
John Gilbert &
Zach Salvatore 24
Founding Families...................... 26

PAGE 12

PAGE 22

PAGE 26

PAGE 29

EPISODE GUIDE

Episode 1: Pilot 30
Episode 2: The Night of the Comet.. 31
Episode 3: Friday Night Bites............. 32
Episode 4: Family Ties 33
Episode 5: You're Undead to Me........ 34
Episode 6: Lost Girls 35
Episode 7: Haunted............................... 36
Episode 8: 162 Candles 37
Episode 9: History Repeating 38
Episode 10: The Turning Point........... 39
Episode 11: Bloodlines 40
Episode 12: Unpleasantville 41
Episode 13: Children of the Damned 42
Episode 14: Fool Me Once................... 43
Episode 15: A Few Good Men............. 44
Episode 16: There Goes the
                      Neighbourhood 45
Episode 17: Let the Right One In 46
Episode 18: Under Control................. 47
Episode 19: Miss Mystic Falls 48
Episode 20: Blood Brothers 49
Episode 21: Isobel 50
Episode 22: Founder's Day 51

THE CAST

Paul Wesley – *Stefan* 54
Ian Somerhalder – *Damon* 55
Nina Dobrev – *Elena/Katherine* ...56
Katerina Graham – *Bonnie*
& **Candice Accola** – *Caroline* 57
Steven R McQueen – *Jeremy*
& **Zach Roerig** – *Matt* 58
Michael Trevino – *Tyler*
& **Kayla Ewell** – *Vicki* 59

Mystic Falls is a sleepy backwater that hides a dark and bloody past

The Beginning

Mystic Falls, Virginia, is a beautiful sleepy backwater town, but hidden in its history lies a dark and murky secret. For centuries, it has been plagued by supernatural incidents and is watched closely by the eyes of the Founders' Council, their prerogative; to keep the town safe from vampires.

The mysterious arrival of two handsome brothers sets in motion a chain of events that threaten to unlock the past and send the town into an unearthly turmoil. As notions of good and evil become twisted, how will their passionate obsession with the beautiful Elena resolve itself? And will their rivalry tear the town apart?

The two mysterious and handsome brothers send the town into an unearthly turmoil

At first sight Stefan appears to be just a regular guy. But there's more to him than meets the eye

STEFAN SALVATORE

Born: 1847, Mystic Falls, Virginia
Age: 162
Father: Giuseppe
Brother: Damon
Eyes: Green
Hair: Light brown
Species: Vampire (only drinks animal blood)
Features: Rose tattoo on his right shoulder
Always carries: A Salvatore signet ring
Residence: The Salvatore Boarding House, run by 'Uncle' Zach Salvatore

When we first meet Stefan Salvatore in modern day Mystic Falls, he appears to be just a regular guy – and the hottest new kid in school. All the girls are struck by his smoulderingly sexy good looks. But Stefan knows there's only one girl in town for him. It's the beautiful Elena Gilbert who, after a chance meeting in the school hallway, is as captivated with him as he is with her. You could call it love at first sight – except Stefan has seen Elena before . . .

Born in 1847 in the Virginian town of Mystic Falls, Stefan led a normal childhood – until the arrival of the beautiful Katherine Pierce (who bears an uncanny resemblance to Elena). A cold and malevolent vampire, Katherine used her powers of mind control and seduction to mould Stefan and his older brother Damon to her will. Both brothers fell completely under her spell and she transformed them into vampires.

Best friends before they were changed, a subsequent incident between the brothers set them against each other as mortal enemies. Now the vengeful Damon is hellbent on destroying Stefan and everything dear to him.

It's not long after Stefan arrives back in Mystic Falls that vicious bloodthirsty attacks start plaguing the town. Could it be possible that they are the work of a determined vampire looking for revenge?

DAMON SALVATORE

Born: 1844, Mystic Falls, Virginia
Age: 166
Father: Giuseppe
Brother: Stefan
Eyes: Blue
Hair: Dark brown
Species: Vampire
Always carries: A Salvatore signet ring
Residence: The Salvatore Boarding House, run by 'Uncle' Zach Salvatore

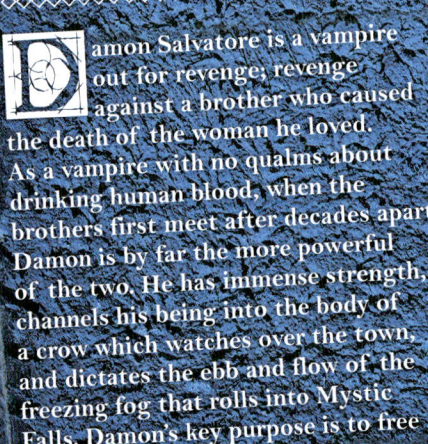

Damon Salvatore is a vampire out for revenge; revenge against a brother who caused the death of the woman he loved. As a vampire with no qualms about drinking human blood, when the brothers first meet after decades apart, Damon is by far the more powerful of the two. He has immense strength, channels his being into the body of a crow which watches over the town, and dictates the ebb and flow of the freezing fog that rolls into Mystic Falls. Damon's key purpose is to free Katherine from the tomb where the Founders' Council trapped her, along with twenty-seven other vampires. But on their release, when he discovers that his love was never imprisoned and had never cared about him, his heart is utterly broken.

Will this vampire realize that the blood ties he thought severed with Stefan can be mended? Will the brothers form a grudging friendship? Can Damon's heart heal when it finds a new object of desire? Even if she turns out to be his brother's girlfriend?

ELENA GILBERT

Born: .... 1992, Mystic Falls, Virginia
Age: 17
Father: .... Grayson Gilbert
Mother: ...... Miranda Gilbert
Aunt: .... Jenna Sommers
Brother: ...... Jeremy
Eyes: .... Brown
Hair: .... Brown

Elena Gilbert's world was turned upside down when her parents were tragically killed in a car accident. Since then, Elena and her younger brother, Jeremy, have been living with their Aunt Jenna. Both brother and sister struggle to cope with the grief. Jeremy starts to go off the rails and although Elena tells everyone she is fine, her best friend Bonnie knows differently.

Then Stefan Salvatore arrives and Elena's life changes for ever. It is clear the pair have an inexplicable attraction to one another. But life in Mystic Falls is never straightforward. Elena begins to suspect that Stefan is hiding a dark and dangerous secret when she discovers news footage of him from 1953 – looking exactly like he does today. Stefan must finally admit what he really is.

Since saving Elena from the car crash that killed her parents, Stefan has been unable to leave Mystic Falls, keen to make sure she is nothing like the malicious Katherine Pierce to whom she bears such an uncanny resemblance . . .

As the mystery of Elena's real parents unfolds (her father is vampire hunter John Gilbert and her mother is the undead Isobel Flemming-Saltzman) it becomes clear that Elena's link to her doppelganger could be more than just skin deep.

KATHERINE PIERCE

The vampire Katherine Pierce entered the lives of Damon and Stefan Salvatore in 1864, during the last throes of the American Civil War. She arrived at the Salvatore Boarding House, travelling as an orphan with her handmaid, Emily Bennett. Using her powers of mind control, she had soon compelled both brothers to fall completely in love with her. Unfortunately, it was Stefan's love that inadvertently led to her banishment from Mystic Falls. When the Founders' Council entombed twenty-seven vampires in the church, Damon believed that Katherine was one of those who had been trapped. He struck a bargain with Emily, asking that she cast a spell to safely protect those vampires who had been entombed. In return he vowed to protect her and all of her descendants. For over 100 years, Damon waits for his chance to open the tomb and free his love. But when the time comes, it seems that Katherine was never trapped at all and has been free to be with Damon – but she has chosen not to find him. She does not love him. But has Katherine's obsession with Mystic Falls and the Salvatore brothers ended . . . or has it only just begun?

Love Bites...

...And nowhere more so than in Mystic Falls. This town is so charged with unearthly and supernatural forces, it's no wonder that the course of true love never did run smooth. Take a look at all the broken hearts and ill-fated romances that have blighted this not-so-sleepy backwater.

ELENA

MATT

Used to date Matt (she dumped him)

Used to date Elena (he is still in love with her)

Lusting after Elena

In love with Stefan

100% infatuated with Elena

Falling in love with Damon?

Now dating

STEFAN

DAMON

KATHERINE

CAROLINE

Once loved Katherine, then she broke his heart

Had a crush on Stefan, but he wasn't interested

Had a fling

Got involved with Damon (he made her a vampire)

JEREMY

ANNA

AUNT JENNA

TYLER

VICKI

JOHN

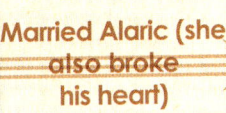
ISOBEL

ALARIC

LOGAN

Met and fell in love with Anna, but she was also a vampire (poor guy) and was staked by his uncle

Loved Jeremy then she got staked

As the typical alpha male he has his eye on all the ladies!

Loved Logan Fell but he broke her heart. He tried to rekindle the flame, but broke her heart for a second time

In love with Vicki, but she broke his heart and became a vampire

Had an on-off relationship with Jeremy

Messed Vicki around. His mom thought she was trash

Had an on-off relationship with Tyler

Now dating

Total love rat. Messed around with Aunt Jenna, then Anna turned him into a vampire before Damon finished him off

Briefly dated John Gilbert. She fell pregnant, gave birth to Elena, who was then adopted by John's brother Grayson and his wife Miranda (she broke John's heart)

Married Alaric (she also broke his heart)

Was married to Isobel Flemming, but she went to the dark side and Damon turned her into a vampire

17

BONNIE BENNETT

Born: 1992
Age: 17
Grandmother: Sheila Bennett
Eyes: Brown
Hair: Brown

Bonnie Bennett is Elena's best friend – and she's the best friend a girl could ever want! She's loyal and would put her life on the line for any of her friends. Although fleetingly attracted to Damon, Bonnie quickly changes her mind about him. Unbeknown to her, she has inherited some of the magical powers passed down from her fourth-great-grandmother, Emily, handmaiden to Katherine Pierce. It is these powers which quickly tell her that Stefan is not all that he seems. Bonnie's skills include clairvoyance, hydrokinesis, pyrokinesis, telekinesis, spell-casting and the ability to cause a vampire pain using the power of her mind. Bonnie soon becomes fully aware of the potency of her powers when her beloved grandmother is killed trying to cast the spell that will open the tomb. She is furious with Stefan, Damon and Elena, and blames them for this misfortune. But how far will this anger take her? Would she ever betray the people she thought had killed her grandmother – especially if it turned out that one of them was her best friend?

CAROLINE FORBES

Born: 1992
Age: 17
Mother: Elizabeth Forbes
Boyfriend: Matt Donovan
Eyes: Blue
Hair: Blonde

Caroline is a bright and cheerful person with an unfortunate tendency to bitchiness. She is very competitive, especially when it comes to Elena, and is constantly trying to impress the other students at Mystic Falls High. Caroline can always be found immaculately dressed, with perfect hair and make-up, but she never seems to get the same success or recognition as Elena and it drives her mad!

Before she hooks up with Matt, she has an unhappy relationship with Damon, which leaves her feeling bruised and used. And although Matt clearly cares for her, their relationship is often strained as he is Elena's ex-boyfriend and will always have very strong feelings for his old flame.

Caroline is completely seduced by Damon's charm

MATT DONOVAN

Born: 1992
Age: 17
Mother: .... Kelly Donovan
Sister: .... Vicki Donovan
Girlfriend: ..... Caroline Forbes
Eyes: .... Blue
Hair: .... Blond

Matt is the all-American boy next door. He's tall and athletic, with blue eyes and blond hair and is Elena's ex-boyfriend. Matt is a loyal, protective and caring person. He shows great concern for the health, welfare and virtue of his sister, Vicki, especially after she is attacked and during her stay in hospital. He is also sure to let Stefan know that he still cares about Elena and would do anything for her. His relationship with both his sister and irresponsible mother has forced him to grow up quickly and become independent, despite his desires to just be a kid.

Matt is a kind-hearted gentleman, who always cares for others over himself

VICKI DONOVAN

Born: 1991
Age: 18
Mother: Kelly Donovan
Brother: Matt Donovan
Boyfriend: Jeremy Gilbert/Tyler Lockwood
Eyes: Brown
Hair: Brown

Vicki is Matt's older sister. Her mother was not around much when she was growing up and she's never really had a strong role model to follow. Matt feels very protective of her and tries his best to stop her life from going off the rails. However, there is no way he can protect her from a ruthless vampire attack.

While walking through the cemetery, Vicki is brutally hurt by Damon. She recovers, but after confessing her weariness with life to Damon, he decides to turn her into a vampire. She completes her transformation when she feeds on Logan Fell, who Damon attacks after the news reporter shoots Stefan with wooden bullets.

Sadly, Vicki has trouble coming to terms with her new existence. When she accidentally bites Jeremy's lip, causing it to bleed, her vampire instincts kick in. She attacks Elena, who steps in to try and protect her brother. Stefan instantly stakes Vicki and her brief time as a vampire comes to a sudden end.

JEREMY GILBERT

Born: 1994
Age: 15
Father: Grayson Gilbert
Mother: Miranda Gilbert
Aunt: Jenna Sommers
Sister: Elena
Eyes: Brown
Hair: Brown

Jeremy used to be a smart, clean-cut, straight-A student. Then his parents were tragically killed and since that day, Jeremy's life has begun to crumble. His grades are slipping, he's straying to the wrong side of the tracks and his on–off relationship with Vicki takes a serious nose-dive when she becomes a vampire. It isn't until Stefan destroys Vicki, and Damon wipes his memory and his pain, that Jeremy starts to rebuild the life he once lived. But this semblance of normality does not last long – when Vicki's body is found, memories of her come flooding back.

His meeting with Anna takes Jeremy down a dark path, where he concludes that the only way to be free of his pain for good is to become a vampire himself.

His heart is broken for a second time when his uncle, John Gilbert, kills Anna, but not before she gives Jeremy a vial of her own blood: drink it, and he will become a vampire. After he hears of her death, Jeremy makes his choice . . . he decides to drink the blood.

TYLER LOCKWOOD

Born: 1992
Age: 17
Father: .... Richard Lockwood
Mother: .... Carol Lockwood
Eyes: .... Brown
Hair: .... Brown

Tyler Lockwood is a bit of a ladies' man. He used to date Vicki, but treated her pretty badly and is now suffering the guilt of never being able to apologize. He also falls out with his best friend, Matt, when he's caught making out with Matt's mom! He's the stereotypical alpha male, which might explain certain mysterious elements of his personality, like the tendency his eyes have to turn yellow, or his weird reaction to John Gilbert's device. But if he's not a vampire, then what is he?

ANNA

Mother: .... Pearl

Anna's mother, Pearl, was one of the twenty-seven vampires entombed under the church, and Anna is in Mystic Falls in a bid to set her free. She believes Jeremy will be able to help her achieve her plan; and he hopes she will turn him into a vampire so he can forget his pain and mental anguish. However, it doesn't take long before they realize their feelings for each other run a little deeper. But just as they discover this, Anna is fatally staked by Founders' Council member, vampire hunter and Jeremy's uncle, John Gilbert.

ALARIC SALTZMAN

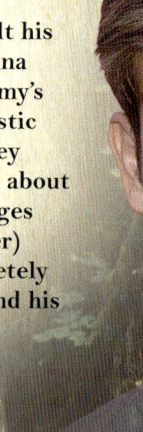

Alaric Saltzman is the replacement history teacher at Mystic Falls High School. He moved to the region with his wife, Isobel, who was investigating mysterious attacks in the Mystic Falls area; attacks she believed were inflicted by a vampire. It seems her investigation uncovered something terrible. One fateful evening, Alaric returned home to find a vampire attacking his wife – that vampire was Damon. Both the vampire and Isobel disappeared, leaving Alaric heartbroken.

Since then he has rebuilt his life and is now dating Jenna Sommers, Elena and Jeremy's aunt. But relations in Mystic Falls are never all that they seem, and when the truth about Elena's real parents emerges (Elena is Isobel's daughter) Alaric is forced to completely re-evaluate his feelings and his place in the town.

Alaric has suffered pain and torment at the hands of vampires

JOHN GILBERT

John Gilbert is the brother of Grayson Gilbert and the true father of Elena. Many years ago John met and fell in love with Isobel Flemming (who would later marry Alaric Saltzman). She fell pregnant, but rather than raise the baby herself, she gave Elena to Grayson and his wife Miranda, who had been trying for a family of their own.

When John realizes that Isobel became a vampire of her own free will, and that it was Damon who turned her, his fury quickly turns to hatred and he vows to destroy all vampires. With the help of the journals left by his ancestor Jonathan Gilbert and the device which can debilitate vampires, John sets out on a rampage that he hopes will rid Mystic Falls of vampires once and for all. But could this vampire hunter's lust for vengeance ultimately bring about his own downfall?

John Gilbert's heart was broken and now it is as hard as stone

ZACH SALVATORE

Zach Salvatore lived in, and was the caretaker of, the Salvatore Boarding House. He was a distant descendant of Damon and Stefan Salvatore, referring to them as 'Uncle' when in private, but posing as *their* uncle in public. Though he trusted Stefan, both Zach and his forefathers lived in fear of Damon. The vampire killed Zach's grandfather, Joseph Salvatore, in 1953. Zach admitted that he avoided starting his own family because of Damon, and grows vervain in the house as protection against him. Zach is brutally killed by Damon after the vampire manages to escape from the Boarding House basement where Zach and Stefan had managed to imprison him. Zach was a member of the Founders' Council and had promised to deliver them the herb, but hadn't fulfilled this when he was killed.

Zach was an honest man who met a brutal end

Founding Families

THE SALVATORES

THE GILBERTS

GIUSEPPE SALVATORE

JONATHAN GILBERT

DAMON SALVATORE

STEFAN SALVATORE

There's a whole host of dark secrets hidden in the Gilberts bloodline

ZACH SALVATORE
DISTANT NEPHEW OF DAMON & STEFAN

UNKNOWN

They may be brothers by blood but in life they're enemies

JENNA SOMMERS

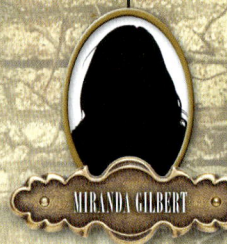
MIRANDA GILBERT

GRAYSON GILBERT

JOHN GILBERT

What does Jenna's future hold for her?

JEREMY GILBERT

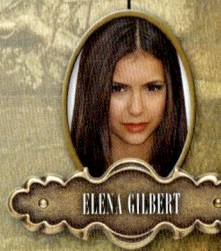
ELENA GILBERT

Blood runs deep in Mystic Falls. Once the town has sunk its teeth into a person, they never leave. Here's a rundown of the family history the town has to offer

THE FORBES
THE LOCKWOODS
THE BENNETS

The Lockwoods take their involvement in the Founders' Council very seriously

- Sheriff William Forbes
- Barnette Lockwood
- Emily Bennett
- Unknown
- Elizabeth Forbes
- Carol Lockwood
- Richard Lockwood
- Sheila Bennett
- Isobel Flemming
- Tyler Lockwood
- Bonnie Bennett
- Caroline Forbes

EPISODE 1
PILOT

Writers: Kevin Williamson and Julie Plec
Director: Marcos Siega

Recently orphaned Elena Gilbert and her brother Jeremy live in Mystic Falls with their aunt Jenna, where they struggle to deal with their parents' tragic car accident four months before. Popular and a straight-A student, Elena turns to writing in her diary in cemeteries to cope with her grief, whilst Jeremy becomes a reckless wildchild.

Elena channels her pain into her diary

Soundtrack:

Contents

- Silversun Pickups – Sort Of
- Mat Kearney – Here We Go
- The Raconteurs – Consoler of the Lonely
- One Republic – Say (All I Need)
- Stars – Take Me to the Riot
- Katy Perry – Thinking of You
- MGMT – Kids
- Placebo – Running Up That Hill
- White Lies – Death
- The All-American Rejects – Back to Me
- Bat For Lashes – Siren Song
- The Fray – Never Say Never

When handsome Stefan Salvatore arrives in town, Elena is drawn to him – but Stefan hides a deadly secret; he is a vampire. Elena's ex-boyfriend Matt grows increasingly jealous and her friend Caroline is also attracted to Stefan, but he is fascinated by Elena – who looks exactly like Katherine, a woman he loved in 1864.

When Matt's sister, Vicki, is attacked and bitten in the woods it seems Stefan is not the only vampire in town. His brother Damon has returned and he and Stefan fight. As Stefan doesn't feed on human blood, Damon is stronger – and so begins a war between good and evil . . . and a war for Elena's soul.

EPISODE 2
THE NIGHT OF THE COMET

Writers: Kevin Williamson and Julie Plec
Director: Marcos Siega
Guest star: Benjamin Ayres

While Vicki recovers in hospital from Damon's attack, Mystic Falls prepares to celebrate a passing comet.

Vicki believes she was attacked by a vampire, so Stefan goes to the hospital to hypnotize her into thinking it was an animal that hurt her, but he is interrupted by Matt.

Jeremy continues to struggle at school, and with his feelings for Vicki, while Aunt Jenna feels that she is failing to be a good surrogate parent for her self-destructive nephew.

Elena visits Stefan at his house, but finds Damon there instead. Damon reveals that Stefan had a relationship with a girl named Katherine, and when Stefan arrives home he doesn't seem pleased to see Elena there.

Vicki's memory of the attack comes back to haunt her and Damon convinces her that it was Stefan who bit her, not him.

Elena goes back to the Salvatore house to see Stefan, and they share their first kiss. Meanwhile, Damon has his sights (and his teeth!) set on Elena's friend Caroline . . .

As the inhabitants of Mystic Falls watch the skies, a vicious predator watches them

Soundtrack:
Metric – Help I'm Alive
Mat Kearney – Closer to Love
The Dead Weather – Hang You from the Heavens
Gossip – Heavy Cross
Neko Case – I'm An Animal
Dragonette – I Get Around
We Were Promised Jetpacks – Conductor
Peaches – Mud
Eastmart – Interloper
Sara Bareilles – Gravity

EPISODE 3
FRIDAY NIGHT BITES

Writers: Barbie Kligman and Bryan M. Holdman
Director: John Dahl
Guest star: Benjamin Ayres

Elena's friend Bonnie has a bad feeling about Stefan, and she's worried about Caroline as she hasn't heard from her for a while. When she arrives at school, Caroline wears a scarf around her neck to cover her bite and tells Elena and Bonnie all about her new boyfriend – Damon.

Trying to humiliate Stefan, Tyler throws a football at him during practice, but it backfires when Stefan's super-speed and strength earn him a place on the football team.

Desperate for Bonnie and Stefan to get along, Elena ignores her friend's psychic vibes, and invites them both for dinner. While they're eating, Damon and Caroline (who he has been feeding off) crash the party. Damon tells Elena about Katherine and how she died in a fire, and she realizes that he also loved her.

At the pre-game pep rally, Stefan gives Elena a necklace filled with vervain (an anti-vampire herb) to protect her from Damon.

Jeremy and Tyler continue to fight over Vicki and Stefan tells Damon that he knows he has some humanity left in him. But this only leads Damon to kill the football coach, Mr Tanner, and Stefan knows that his brother must be stopped.

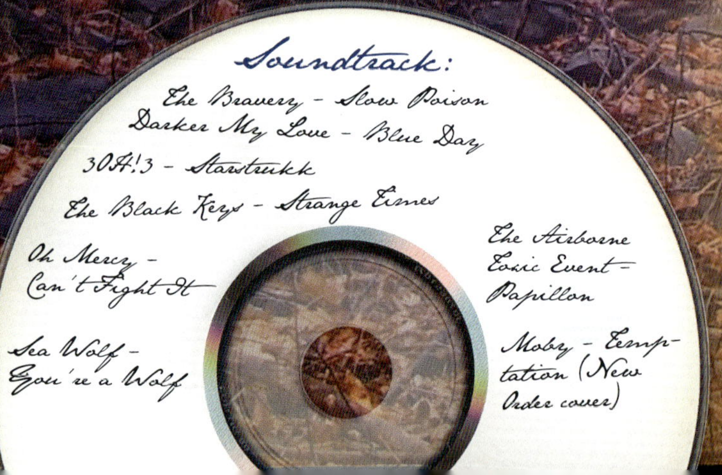

Soundtrack:
The Bravery – Slow Poison
Darker My Love – Blue Day
30H!3 – Starstrukk
The Black Keys – Strange Times
Oh Mercy – Can't Fight It
Sea Wolf – You're a Wolf
The Airborne Toxic Event – Papillon
Moby – Temptation (New Order cover)

EPISODE 4
FAMILY TIES

Writers: Andrew Kreisberg and Brian Young
Director: Guy Ferland
Guest star: Chris William Martin

s Stefan doesn't drink human blood, Damon can enter his dreams and plant a nightmare where the evil vampire kills Elena.

Meanwhile, Stefan's 'Uncle' Zach tells him that he's been growing vervain in the basement and that they can stop Damon by poisoning him with the deadly herb. Stefan tries to spike Damon's drink with it, but he fails and it only angers Damon.

Elena asks Stefan to escort her to the annual Founders' Party and Vicki gets Tyler to invite her.

Elena tries to question Stefan about his past, but he's unresponsive and cagey. She runs off and bumps into Caroline, noticing the bite marks and bruises on her neck and back.

Stefan puts vervain in Caroline's champagne, so Damon collapses after he drinks her blood and Stefan drags him away, locking him up in the basement of the Salvatore Boarding House. Weakened by the vervain, Damon cannot escape.

Soundtrack:
Union of Knives – Opposite Direction
Santigold – I'm a Lady
Carolina Liar – I'm Not Over
Thievery Corporation – Shadows of Ourselves
VV Brown – Back in Time
Sofi Bonde – Fallout
Glass Pear – Wild Place
Matt Nathanson – All We Are
The Submarines – Brightest Hour (Morgan Page Remix)
Viva Voce – Believer

Damon's evil plans are put on hold when his brother manages to infect his blood with vervain

EPISODE 5
YOU'RE UNDEAD TO ME

Writers: Sean Reycraft and Gabrielle Stanton
Director: Kevin Bray
Guest star: Jasmine Guy

Stefan plans on leaving Damon locked up in the basement with the vervain while he slowly starves and loses all his strength.

Jeremy and Vicki have got back together, and with his brother imprisoned, Stefan sets about saving his relationship with Elena. He opens up to her and tells her more about himself and about Katherine, but when Elena cuts herself he has to hide his vampire instincts and she becomes suspicious.

At a school charity car wash to raise money after the death of Mr Tanner, Bonnie discovers that she has powers she didn't know she possessed when she accidentally sets a car on fire. Confused, she goes to her grandmother for help.

Elena meets an old man who swears he saw Stefan in 1953, and so she begins to investigate.

Meanwhile, Damon still has a hold over Caroline and he lures her to the basement to release him. When Zach tries to stop her, Damon breaks his neck.

Elena locates some footage from a 1950s Salvatore news story, she sees that her boyfriend hasn't aged a day. As she goes to confront Stefan, Damon is hungry for blood and gets his fill when he attacks Vicki in the woods.

Stefan struggles to hide his vampire instincts when exposed to Elena's blood

Soundtrack:
S.O. Stereo - When a Heart Breaks
Howie Day - Be There
30H!3 - Don't Trust Me
Gabriella Cilmi - Save the Lies
Anjulie - Boom
Mads Langer - Beauty of the Dark

EPISODE 6
LOST GIRLS

Writers: Kevin Williamson and Julie Plec
Director: Marcos Siega
Guest stars: Marguerite MacIntyre, Rob Pralgo

Soundtrack:
- A Fine Frenzy – Stood Up
- Editors – Weight of the World
- The Temper Trap – Fader
- Anberlin – Enjoy the Silence (Depeche Mode cover)
- Green Day – 21 Guns
- Jason Walker – Down

Stefan's secret is out – Elena knows the truth about him and Damon. Stefan tells her the story of how he became a vampire and how his rivalry with Damon began during the Civil War when they both fell in love with Katherine, the vampire who sired them.

Stefan tells Elena that he has been seventeen years old since he became a vampire in 1864. Katherine turned Damon, and glamoured the two brothers so that they wouldn't tell the other.

While Stefan is out, Damon revives Vicki by feeding her his blood and initiating her change into a vampire. Scared, Vicki runs to Jeremy, but he thinks she's on drugs and calls Matt.

When Elena and Stefan return, Stefan realizes what has happened and goes to find Vicki. He tries to talk to her and teach her not to feed on humans, but news reporter Logan is hunting vampires with Sheriff Forbes, and he shoots Stefan with a wooden bullet. Before Logan can stake Stefan, Damon saves him and Vicki feeds off Logan, completing her transformation.

EPISODE 7
HAUNTED

Writer: Andrew Kreisberg
Director: Ernest Dickenson
Guest star: Jasmine Guy

Vicki's bloodlust is growing and while Stefan tries to teach her how to control her hunger and feast on the blood of animals, Damon wants her to be more like him, showing her how to move at superhuman speed. She runs away from the brothers and goes home to find Matt, resisting the urge to drink her own brother's blood.

Bonnie discovers more about her past and is told by her grandmother that her family were witches who lived during the time of the Salem Witch Trials, leaving the area in the late 1690s.

Plagued by misery and addiction, Vicki's short life meets a tragic end.

At school, Caroline gives Bonnie a witch costume for the school's Halloween party and a necklace she took from Damon – the necklace had once belonged to Bonnie's fourth-great grandmother.

At the party, volatile Vicki is dressed up as a vampire. As she kisses Jeremy, she bites him on the lip and starts to suck his blood. But when Stefan and Elena confront Vicki, she bites Elena on the neck and Stefan drives a stake through her heart.

Jeremy is distraught, and Elena asks Stefan to wipe her brother's memory to take away the pain. Stefan is not strong enough, and so Damon is called upon to do it for them.

Soundtrack:

Contents

Gary Go – Open Arms
Final Flash – Fading Light
The Sounds – No One Sleeps When I'm Awake
White Lies – To Lose My Life
The Longcut – Open Hearts
The Dodos – Fables
Bat For Lashes – Sleep Alone
Sanders Bohlke – The Weight of Us

EPISODE 8
162 CANDLES

Writers: Barbie Kligman and Gabrielle Stanton
Director: Rick Bota
Guest stars: Arielle Kebbel

It's Stefan's birthday and he is surprised by a visit from one of his oldest friends, 350 year-old vampire, Lexi.

Elena is worried about Jeremy. Ever since Damon erased his memory of Vicki, he has been doing his homework and staying away from drugs, but what other side effects might arise from Damon's brainwashing?

Bonnie visits Elena and tells her about *her* powers, but Elena hides Stefan's secret from her. She is adamant that she and Stefan can't be together – he is a vampire, after all – but when she goes to see him and bumps into Lexi, the other vampire gives her some relationship advice.

Damon commits a treacherous act

Damon is not pleased to see Lexi. Far older than him, she is also much stronger. He kills a young guy and compels his girlfriend into telling the police that it was Lexi who attacked them. Sheriff Forbes injects Lexi with vervain and when she tries to escape, Damon stakes her – all part of helping control the 'vampire problem', and convincing the Sheriff that Damon isn't a vampire.

Soundtrack:

The Birthday Massacre – Happy Birthday
Pete Yorn – Thinking Of You
Fresto feat. Tegan & Sara – Feel It In My Bones
Telekinesis – Tokyo
Mike Sheridan and Mads Langer – Too Close
Fauxliage – All The World
The Black Box Revelation – Love In Your Head
Switchfoot – Yet

EPISODE 9
HISTORY REPEATING

Writers: Bryan M Holdman and Brian Young
Director: Marcos Siega
Guest stars: Matt Davis, Bianca Lawson

When new history teacher Alaric Saltzman arrives in town, Jeremy takes a liking to him and introduces him to his Aunt Jenna. But the newcomer wears a ring like Damon and Stefan, and pauses at Jenna's front door after their date.

Meanwhile, Bonnie is experiencing very vivid and terrifying dreams about her ancestor, Emily. Damon tries to claim the necklace from her, but she can't seem to get rid of it. Since Damon compelled her, Caroline has been trying to steal the amulet, and she and Bonnie continue to argue over it.

Is new history teacher Alaric all that he seems?

Elena, Bonnie and Caroline decide to have a séance to contact Emily, but the lights go out and the necklace vanishes. Bonnie finds it in the bathroom and she becomes possessed by Emily before her friends can reach her. Damon finally reveals to Stefan the real reason he has come back to Mystic Falls – to resurrect Katherine, using the amulet.

Stefan tries to stop Damon as he knows that the vampires in Old Fell's church were burned to death by the townspeople, and that they will take their revenge on the new generation of townspeople as a penalty.

When Damon goes for the crystal again, Bonnie/Emily uses her power to throw him onto to the branch of a tree. Then Emily performs the ritual to destroy the crystal, and releases Bonnie from her possession.

Soundtrack:
Echo & The Bunnymen – Think I Need It Too
Pablo Sebastian – Lies
Idlewild – Post Electric
The Bravery – The Spectator
Great Northern – Houses
Barcelona – Come Back When You Can

EPISODE 10
THE TURNING POINT

Writers: Kevin Williamson, Julie Plec and Barbie Kligman
Director: J Miller Tobin
Guest stars: Marguerite MacIntyre, Matt Davis and Rob Pralgo

Logan Fell is back in town . . . but not in human form! A bona fide vampire, he attacks and kills several people. Damon offers to help the sheriff find who is responsible for the murders and tracks Logan down. He demands to know who turned Logan, but Logan says he doesn't know and shoots him with a wooden bullet. Leaving Damon for dead, Logan kidnaps Caroline.

Stefan and Damon now have a common enemy in Logan and come together to save Caroline. They fight, and Logan tells the brothers that they are not the only people who want to know how to get into the tomb. Damon agrees to meet Logan at the church tomb later that night to find out more, but when Logan arrives at the warehouse, Alaric is waiting for him. It transpires that Alaric is not a vampire, but a vampire hunter!

After Stefan has taken Caroline home, Elena tells him that she loves him but she becomes frightened when she sees an old photograph of Katherine. Upset, she drives away so quickly that she hits a man and her car rolls over, trapping her inside. When the person she hit gets up and starts to walk towards her, she soon realizes that he isn't human . . .

FANG FACT!
STEFAN WANTED TO BE A DOCTOR BEFORE HE TURNED INTO A VAMPIRE, BUT HE COULDN'T BECAUSE OF THE BLOOD

Soundtrack:
Five For Fighting - Chances
Telekinesis - Coast of Carolina
The Features - Off Track
Plumb - Cut
Tyrone Wells - This Is Beautiful

EPISODE 11
BLOODLINES

Writers: Kevin Williamson and Julie Plec
Director: Dave Barrett
Guest stars: Gina Torres, Jasmine Guy and Malese Jow

Trapped in her car, Elena is rescued by Damon and the figure disappears. The vampire carries her away, and when she awakens, he tells her they are going to Georgia.

Despite Elena's protests, Damon takes her to meet his old flame, Bree, who is a barmaid and a witch.

Elena refuses to answer Stefan's calls as she is still freaked out by her own likeness to Katherine, so a worried Stefan goes to Bonnie for help to find her. Bonnie overcomes her fears of her powers but is sucked into the ground outside the tomb where Katherine is buried. Stefan finds her and flies her to safety.

Damon goes to Bree to ask how he can get into Katherine's tomb, but Bree says they cannot open it without Emily's crystal. She places a call and Lee, Lexi's vampire boyfriend, arrives. He wants revenge on Damon.

Lee attacks Damon, but Elena begs for his life. Lee spares Damon, but Damon then kills Bree for betraying him.

When Elena gets home she confronts Stefan. He tells her he saved her from the crash when her parents' car went over the bridge, and that when he looked into her family history, he found out that she was adopted.

Bonnie is brave enough to use her powers, but finds herself in danger

Soundtrack:

- Florence & The Machine – Cosmic Love
- Editors – An End Has A Start
- The Dandelions – On A Mission
- Black Mustang – Between the Devil and the Deep Blue Sea
- The Black Hollies – Can't Stop These Tears (From Falling)
- Hope Sandoval and The Warm Inventions – Trouble
- The Steps – Push
- The Upsidedown – Pepper Spray
- The Stereotypes – The Night Before
- The Dig – Look Inside
- Alex Band – Only One
- Julian Casablancas – Out Of The Blue
- The Bell – Nothing Is Logical

EPISODE 12
UNPLEASANTVILLE

Writers: Barbie Kligman and Brian Young
Director: Liz Friedlander
Guest stars: Matt Davis, Dillon Casey and Malese Jow

Stefan and Damon try to figure out who the new vampire in town could be – the one that Elena hit with her car. He seems to be following her and he knows her phone number.

Stefan gives Elena more vervain-filled jewellery to protect her family and friends while she continues to investigate her true origins.

She confronts her aunt Jenna about her adoption and discovers that a pregnant sixteen-year-old turned up at Elena's father's hospital. Dr Gilbert altered the birth certificate and he and Mrs Gilbert adopted Elena without telling anyone she wasn't their own child.

Needing to make some money, Matt takes a job at the Mystic Grill, where former high school football star Ben works. When Bonnie is harassed by Damon, Ben goes to her aid.

At the school dance, the mysterious vampire, Noah, attacks Elena and threatens to kill Jeremy. Stefan and Damon stake him, but before he dies he reveals that the way to get into the tomb and reach Katherine can be found in Jonathan Gilbert's journal.

While Jenna and Alaric are walking home from the party, Alaric tells Jenna that his wife was named Isobel, the same name as Elena's birth mother. Meanwhile, Anna tries to get close to Jeremy because she wants to get her hands on his ancestor's journal. We find out that both Anna and Ben are vampires, and they seem to be a couple.

The key to accessing Katherine's tomb is finally revealed – it's in Jonathan's journal

Soundtrack:

We Barbarians – There's This There's That
Systems Officer – Pacer
The Misfits – This Magic Moment
Rogue Wave – Everyday
Jef Scot – Dreams Are For The Lucky
M.S. Royalty – Keep It Cool (Bo Flex Remix)
The Misfits – Runaway
Autovaughn – Everybody
Jacko Marcellino – Slow Dance
The Misfits – Great Balls Of Fire
The Raveonettes – My Boyfriend's Back
St. Leonards – Now That We've Grown
Oranger – Mr. Sandman

41

EPISODE 13
CHILDREN OF THE DAMNED

Writers: Kevin Williamson and Julie Plec
Director: Marcos Siega
Guest stars: Matt Davis and Sean Faris

This is the second major flashback episode so far. We find out what caused the rift between Stefan and Damon all those many years ago. It was Stefan who accidentally revealed that Katherine was a vampire to his father – one of the town's vampire slayers. Damon blames his brother for betraying Katherine, and in turn, for her imprisonment.

In the present-day plot, Jeremy tells Stefan, Elena and Damon that he gave the journal to Alaric, and that his new friend Anna also has a strong interest in it.

When Stefan confronts Alaric, he discovers that the Alaric is hunting Damon because he saw him kill his wife, but her body was never found. When they go to get the journal, it has gone. Alaric had made photocopies, and when Elena and Stefan read it, they deduce that the grimoire (Emily's spell book) has been buried with Stefan's father – so they dig him up to retrieve it.

Meanwhile, Damon goes with Jeremy to meet Anna, and recognizes her as the daughter of Pearl – a woman he knew in 1864. When Damon confronts her, she confesses to turning both Ben and Logan into vampires. She stole the journal so that she could open the tomb and rescue her mother.

The episode ends with Damon feeding Elena his blood so that Stefan will give him the grimoire. When Stefan takes Elena back to her house, she is later kidnapped by Anna. Poor Elena!

Stefan has to open his father's grave to recover Emily's spell book

Soundtrack:

Kate Earl - When You're Ready
Surfer Blood - Floating Vibes
Elefant - Goodbye
Experimental Aircraft - Stellar

EPISODE 14
FOOL ME ONCE

Writer: Brett Conrad
Director: Marcos Siega
Guest stars: Jasmine Guy and Malese Jow

Elena and Bonnie have both been kidnapped by vampires Anna and Ben. With help from Grams, Stefan finds the girls using a locator spell and orders Ben to leave town.

Elena, Stefan and Bonnie decide to help Damon free Katherine, and they convince Grams to go with them to the tomb and help them open it. Bonnie and Grams succeed, but unbeknown to Damon they leave the seal on, keeping the vampires inside and preventing any from escaping.

Anna and Ben arrive and Stefan kills Ben for not obeying his orders. Anna uses Jeremy as leverage, and Damon uses Elena to make sure they don't close the tomb on him. But when

Bonnie works with Gram to trap the vampires

Stefan hears Elena scream, he rushes in after her.

Anna has torn Elena's arm open to feed her mother Pearl, and Bonnie forces Grams to temporarily lift the seal – Stefan and Damon make it out, but so do Anna and Pearl . . . and perhaps someone else?

Damon is distraught that he didn't find Katherine and when he later confronts Anna, learns that she turned a church guard into a vampire in 1864 and has been free the whole time. Anna tells him that she last saw Katherine in 1983 and that she has had no interest in looking for Damon.

The episode ends on an even sadder note, when Grams passes away – the powerful spells taking too much out of her.

Soundtrack:

Oh Mercy – Can't Fight It
Earlimart – Before It Gets Better
The Soft Pack – Answer To Yourself
Tokyo Police Club – In a Cave
M. S. Royalty – Every Summer
The Steps – Out Tonight
Black Rebel Motorcycle Club – All You Do Is Talk
Leona Lewis – Run (Snow Patrol cover)

EPISODE 15
A FEW GOOD MEN

Writer: Brian Young
Director: Joshua Butler
Guest star: Marguerite MacIntyre

Harper, the vampire that escaped from the tomb, attacks a man in the wood and changes into his clothes.

Matt and Caroline are surprised by the return of Matt's mother, Kelly, while Aunt Jenna has discovered that Isobel Flemming, from Grove Hill, Virginia, gave up Elena for adoption when she was in high school. Jenna then gives Elena the address of Isobel's best friend, Trudie Peterson.

Elena goes to find Trudie, who tells her a bit about her mother, but she's hiding something. Trudie texts 'SHE'S HERE' to someone, and gives Elena vervain tea.

When Elena realizes, Trudie asks her to leave. As she's getting into her car, Elena sees a man watching her. He then enters Trudie's house and kills her.

Jenna tells Alaric that Elena's mother and his presumed-dead wife are the same – and Damon happily admits to killing her.

Elena hears this and runs away (followed by Stefan), but she sees the stranger from Trudie's house. He tells her that Isobel doesn't want to see her. Then he is hit by a truck, and Elena steals his phone.

She calls the most recently-dialled number and asks, 'Isobel?', but the woman hangs up.

Damon tells Alaric that he turned Isobel into a vampire and then stakes him. But thanks to an enchanted ring that Isobel gave him, Alaric survives.

Elena begins to suspect her real mother is still alive

Soundtrack:

Jet - Black Hearts (On Fire)
The Alternate Routes - Time Is A Runaway
Sound Team - Your Eyes Are Liars
Above The Golden State - Real You
Sweet Thing - Winter Night
Free Energy - Something In Common
Sounds Under Radio - Portrait Of A Summer Thief

EPISODE 16
THERE GOES THE NEIGHBOURHOOD

Writer: Bryan Oh and Andrew Chambliss
Director: Kevin Bray
Guest star: Melinda Clarke

When Caroline asks Stefan and Elena to double-date with her and Matt to prove they can all be friends, the first word that comes to mind is 'awkward'. Stefan thinks it's a 'great idea', but Caroline ends up regretting it when Matt and Elena reminisce about old times, and Matt and Stefan bond over classic cars.

We discover that Pearl and Anna have been hiding out in a farmhouse outside town with a large number of hungry vampires. They have escaped from the tomb and are looking for revenge.

Anna and Pearl demand from Damon a list of people in the town council that he has been supplying with vervain. He is promised Katherine's location as a reward. Pearl attacks him when he refuses.

Jeremy has been online, asking questions about how someone can become a vampire. Anna really likes Jeremy, but when she visits, he deliberately cuts himself to see how she reacts. Now that he knows what Anna is, she asks him to keep her true form a secret... and he asks her to turn him into a vamp.

Soundtrack:
Keane - Better Than This
In-Flight Safety - CloudHead
Tegan & Sara - The Ocean
Marianas Trench - Cross My Heart
The Constellations - Perfect Day
In-Flight Safety - Crash
Erin McCarley - Lovesick Mistake
Parachute - The Mess I Made

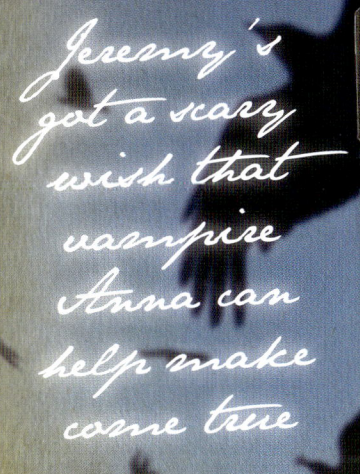

Jeremy's got a scary wish that vampire Anna can help make come true

EPISODE 17
LET THE RIGHT ONE IN

Writer: Julie Plec with a story by Brian Young
Director: Dennis Smith
Guest star: Melinda Clarke

Jeremy continues to ask Anna to turn him into a vampire, but she refuses. She even tells him to keep the bracelet that Elena gave him for protection.

Despite Pearl's warnings, Stefan is kidnapped by Frederick and some rogue vampires who are hell-bent on revenge. When Damon goes after him, he cannot enter the house they are torturing Stefan in, because they refuse to invite him in.

Damon tells Elena and they go to Alaric for help. Armed with vervain darts, Alaric enters the vampire house under the pretext of using the phone. When Stefan is rescued, Elena feeds him her blood for strength, but Stefan has not had human blood in a very long time . . . and he seems to really enjoy it.

When Caroline's car breaks down in a storm, she literally stumbles upon Vicki's rotten corpse.

Anna agrees to turn Jeremy, but when the sheriff tells Matt that Vicki's body has been found, Jeremy is distraught. Anna realizes that the only reason Jeremy wanted to be a vampire was so that he could be with Vicki. He doesn't deny it.

Anna finally discovers Jeremy's real reason for wanting to become a vampire

Soundtrack:
Class Actress – Let Me Take You Out
The Morning Benders – I Was Wrong
The Silent League – Resignation Studies
The Black Angels – Young Men Dead
Lights On – Bory
Love Grenades – Young Lovers (Sam Sparrow Mix)
Systems Officer – East
Black Rebel Motorcycle Club – Conscience Killer
Sounds Under Radio – All You Wanted

EPISODE 18
UNDER CONTROL

Writer: Barbie Kligman and Andrew Chambliss
Director: David Von Ancken
Guest stars: Malese Jow, Melinda Clarke, and David Anders

After his human blood intake, Stefan becomes insatiable and tries to detox himself. Damon enjoys watching him struggle, and tries to convince him to drink to keep up his strength, but Stefan is insistent that he'll be OK.

Elena and Jeremy's uncle, John Gilbert, shows up in town – and no one seems particularly pleased to see him. There is immediate tension between John and Jenna, and she senses that he has ulterior motives for coming to visit.

At the Founder's Day kick-off event, Stefan is not himself. He copes with his bloodlust by getting drunk and becomes very angry and aggressive.

John tells Damon that he knows about the tomb and the vampires that have escaped from it. Damon snaps John's neck and throws him off the roof. But before you can say 'John's your dead uncle', he's back at the party – fit as a fiddle! Damon notices a ring on John's hand that is just like the one Alaric has.

Jeremy finds Elena's diary and reads the entry about Vicki's death. He also discovers that Damon deliberately removed his memory of the event.

John Gilbert arrives in town for a visit, but no one is very glad to see him back

Soundtrack:

Black Mustang – You and I
The Golden Dogs – Yeah!
Phoenix – 1901
The Postelles – White Night
Katy Perry – Use Your Love
Paramore – Brick By Boring Brick
The Virgins – Hey Hey Girl
The Airborne Toxic Event – Does This Mean You're Moving On?
The Morning After Girls – To Be Your Loss

47

EPISODE 19
MISS MYSTIC FALLS

Writers: Bryan Oh and Caroline Dries
Director: Marcos Siega
Guest stars: Autumn Dial, Spencer Locke, David Anders

Anna goes to see Damon on behalf of her mother. She apologizes for what the other rogue vampires did to Stefan and says that they tried to overthrow Pearl. Damon tells her that she and the other vampires need to stop robbing the blood bank, but Anna claims that she hasn't been there in over a week and that the other vampires have left town. Damon confronts Stefan about drinking human blood, but he denies it.

Stefan abandons Elena at the Miss Mystic Falls ceremony, forcing Damon to step in as her escort. Meanwhile, Stefan has abducted Amber, one of the pageant contestants, and is battling with himself over whether to feed on her. He decides that he will, but is interrupted by Damon and Elena. Stefan attacks his brother as he tries to stop him, but Bonnie arrives and uses her powers to give Stefan a searing pain in his head, and he runs away.

When Stefan returns home, Pearl and Anna are waiting for him. Pearl gives Damon the invention that John wants.

Elena goes to see Stefan. He tries to scare her away but she knows he is not well. She injects him with vervain and then she and Damon lock him up to detox.

Stefan's blood-lust is so strong that he can no longer control it on his own

Soundtrack:

Contents

Faber Drive – Never Coming Down
Johann Strauss Jr. – On The Beautiful Blue Danube
Vitamin String Quartet – Yellow (The String Quartet Tribute To Coldplay)
Vitamin String Quartet – Clocks (The String Quartet Tribute To Coldplay)
Luigi Boccherini – Menuet Célèbre
Within Temptation – All I Need

EPISODE 20
BLOOD BROTHERS

Writers: Kevin Williamson and Julie Plec
Director: Liz Friedlander
Guest stars: Kelly Hu, David Anders, Malese Jow

Stefan is locked up in a cell as Elena and Damon try to cure him of his human blood addiction. But he's refusing to even drink animal blood, and in his withdrawal delirium, finds himself thinking of the past. Through his flashbacks, we discover that when Damon and Stefan tried to rescue Katherine, their own father shot them for siding with a vampire.

Elena finds it difficult to see Stefan in so much pain. He tries to scare her into leaving, but she stands her ground. He says he's making the decision he should have made years ago, and then tells the story of his original transition — completed when he fed on his own father's blood.

We discover that it was Stefan who urged Damon to become a vampire, even bringing him a young girl to feed on.

Stefan's guilt over how many people he has hurt since they both became vampires is the reason he is starving himself. Escaping from the cell, he goes out without his ring in an attempt to kill himself when the sun comes up. Elena talks him round, her trust in and love for him constant.

John Gilbert stakes Pearl as she prepares to leave town, and the episode ends with the infamous Isobel returning.

Soundtrack:

Timbaland with One Republic – Marchin On (Timbo Version)
Little Boots – Click
Robert Skoro – In Line
Jamie McDonald – I'll Be Thinking of You
Aron Wright – Song for the Waiting
We The Kings – We'll Be A Dream

Stefan feels so guilty for all the pain he has caused

EPISODE 21
ISOBEL

Writers: Caroline Dries and Brian Young
Director: J Miller Tobin
Guest stars: Mia Kirshner, David Anders and Malese Jow

Isobel is back, and to Alaric's horror, there's very little of the woman he once loved left. She has become utterly consumed by her new life as a vampire. She forces Alaric to arrange a meeting with her daughter, Elena. Elena is desperate to find out the identity of her real father, but all she uncovers is the terrifying truth that if she doesn't retrieve Jonathan Gilbert's device from Damon, her deranged mother will embark on a killing spree in Mystic Falls.

Fearful of the effect the

Elena finally has her first meeting with her mother

device will have, Elena convinces Bonnie to place a charm on the machine that will render it useless. However, unbeknown to Elena, Bonnie's spell was a fake and the device remains deadly. But nothing is ever what it seems in Mystic Falls. Isobel and John Gilbert are actually working together to recover Jonathan Gilbert's device as part of Katherine's orders. The plan will culminate in the use of the device to kill all the vampires trapped in the tomb, as well as Damon and Stefan. But why would John want to associate with Isobel? They used to be lovers ... and so the truth about Elena's real father becomes clear. And why would Isobel want to kill her own kind, including Stefan and her maker, Damon? Could this be her way of trying to protect her daughter from following the fate of her mother? As Isobel leaves Mystic Falls, she wipes herself from Alaric's memory, thus finally healing his broken heart.

Soundtrack:
- Vampire Weekend – Giving Up The Gun
- Anya Marina – All The Same To Me
- Neon Trees – Our War
- Sounds Under Radio – Sing
- Cage The Elephant – Ain't No Rest For The Wicked
- The Cribs – We Share The Same Skies
- Band Of Horses – Laredo

EPISODE 22
FOUNDER'S DAY

Writers: Bryan Oh & Andrew Chambliss
Director: Marcos Siega
Guest stars: David Anders, Malese Jow and Robert Pralgo

It's Founder's Day in Mystic Falls and preparations for the party are in full swing. Anna confides in Jeremy that it was his Uncle John who killed her mother and asks him to leave Mystic Falls with her, giving him a vial of her blood and explaining how he can use it to become a vampire himself.

As the floats roll down the main street, Damon thanks Bonnie for deactivating John Gilbert's device, but Bonnie knows it will still work.

John Gilbert reveals his strange machine and plan to the Founders' Council. Once it is on, all vampires will be struck down and the sheriff's men will be able to inject them with vervain, incapacitating them long enough to herd them into the Gilbert Building to be burned.

John activates the device and the vampires of Mystic Falls are paralysed with pain. The police round them up, including Anna, Damon and Mayor Lockwood. Tyler Lockwood also feels the effects. He crashes his car and the paramedic attending him witnesses his eyes turn yellow.

Stefan races to the Gilbert Building to save Damon. Bonnie enchants him so he can enter the basement and free his brother. Stefan and Elena return to school, while Damon goes to tell Jeremy about Anna. Elena arrives home just as Damon is leaving and the tension between them is so strong that they kiss. Elena confronts John and, furious, grabs a kitchen knife and slices off his ring finger. Dying, he finally realizes that Katherine has returned.

Every vampire in Mystic Falls is in terrible danger

Soundtrack:
Ellie Goulding – Every Time You Go
Sia – You've Changed
Lifehouse – It Is What It Is
Anberlin – True Faith (New Order cover)
Stateless – Bloodstream (DVD Mix)

52

The Cast

PAUL WESLEY
STEFAN SALVATORE

Name: Paul Thomas Wasilewski (screen name - Paul Wesley)
Born: 23 July 1982
From: New Brunswick, New Jersey

Paul Wesley was born Paul Thomas Wasilewski to Polish parents Agnieszka and Tomasz Wasilewski. He grew up in Marlboro, New Jersey, and has one older sister, Monika, and two younger sisters, Julia and Leah.

Wesley landed his first acting role as Max Nickerson in *Guiding Light* while he was in his junior year at high school. He transferred from Marlboro High School to Lakewood Prep School in Howell, New Jersey to accommodate his busy acting schedule. After graduation, Paul started college at Rutgers University in New Jersey, but left after one semester with his parents' support when he realized he could make a career out of acting straight away.

LIKES
Ice hockey, snowboarding

WHERE HAVE YOU SEEN HIM BEFORE?
Law & Order: Criminal Intent, Smallville, The O.C., CSI: Miami, Shark, 24

On changing his name:
'My birthname is too hard to pronounce! I asked my family's permission to change it, and it's really helped my career.'

FIVE FAVOURITES
TV SHOW – Six Feet Under
FOOD – Sushi
SONG – 'Melatonin', Silversun Pickups
COLOUR – Blue
ACTRESS – Monica Bellucci

DID YOU KNOW?
Paul didn't go to his high school prom. Apparently 'Girls didn't like me that much'

IAN SOMERHALDER
DAMON SALVATORE

Name: .... Ian Joseph Somerhalder
Born: .... 8 December 1978
From: .... Covington, Louisiana

Ian Somerhalder was born in Covington, Louisiana, the son of Edna Somerhalder and Robert Somerhalder, who worked in building construction. He has a brother, Bob, who was once a professional cyclist, and a sister, Robin, who is a broadcast journalist. One of Somerhalder's first roles was as Hamilton Fleming in the short-lived TV series *Young Americans*, a spin-off of *Dawson's Creek*. It was in 2002 that Somerhalder landed the role of Paul Denton in Roger Avery's adaptation of Bret Easton Ellis' novel, *The Rules of Attraction*, alongside James Van Der Beek and Jessica Biel. Somerhalder's next big break came in 2004 when he was one of the first actors to be cast in hit TV series *Lost*. He played Boone Carlyle in the show. Then in 2006 he was recognized for his smouldering good looks when he was named one of DNA Models' Top 10 Male Models.

FIVE FAVOURITES
- FOOD – Mince pies
- SONG – '15 Step', Radiohead
- COLOUR – Turquoise
- ACTOR – Sean Penn
- MOVIE – The Graduate

LIKES
Yoga, baseball, horseriding, archery, football and cycling

IF HE WASN'T AN ACTOR
'I'd probably be a marine biologist'

WHERE HAVE YOU SEEN HIM BEFORE?
Lost, CSI: Miami, Smallville

What's the difference between Stefan and Damon's dating styles?

'Well, Stefan would work hard to not have to use mind compulsion on a girl. Damon, after literally ten minutes, would go "forget it" and grab her and say "you want me" and that would be it.'

DID YOU KNOW?
Somerhalder began modelling at the age of ten

NINA DOBREV
ELENA GILBERT/KATHERINE PIERCE

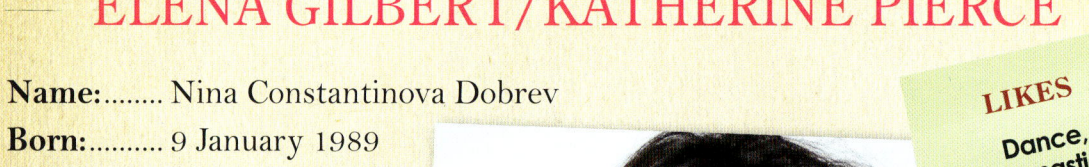

Name: Nina Constantinova Dobrev
Born: 9 January 1989
From: Sofia, Bulgaria

Dobrev was born in Sofia, Bulgaria and moved to Canada at the age of two, where she was raised in Toronto, Ontario. Her mother is an artist while her father is a computer specialist. She has one older brother, Aleksander, who is studying to become an engineer. Modelling jobs led to commercials, which then turned into film auditions, but it's her role in *The Vampire Diaries* that has catapulted Nina into the limelight.

LIKES
Dance, gymnastics, theatre, music, visual arts, and acting

DID YOU KNOW?
Nina is a talented gymnast who has represented Canada in competitions around the world

Funniest moment on set?
'There are so many. One of the best was when we were filming the 1864 stuff and I was Katherine. I was running and turned round to look at who was following me and tripped over my skirt. Because it had a hoop in it the whole thing went over my head.'

FIVE FAVOURITES
FOOD – Chocolate
SONG – 'For The Nights I Can't Remember', Hedley
COLOUR – Black
BOOK – The Lovely Bones
MOVIE – The Notebook

KATERINA GRAHAM
BONNIE BENNETT

Name:........ Katerina Alexandre Graham
Born:.......... 5 September 1989
From:......... Geneva, Switzerland

In her short years, Graham has turned her hand to pretty much everything! She has worked as an actress, singer, record producer, dancer and model. Born in Geneva, Switzerland, Graham is the daughter of a Liberian father, Joseph Graham, and a Russian mother, Natasha. She grew up in Los Angeles and speaks English, Spanish, French, some Portuguese and Hebrew.

DID YOU KNOW?
Graham is the voice behind will.i.am's single 'I Got It From My Mama'. In 2010, Graham appeared in Justin Bieber's and Usher's music video, 'Somebody to Love' (Remix)

CANDICE ACCOLA
CAROLINE FORBES

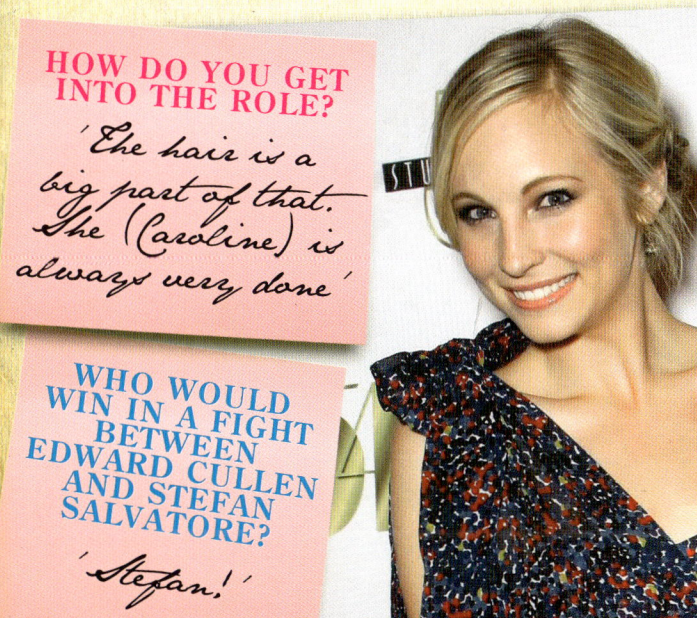

HOW DO YOU GET INTO THE ROLE?
'The hair is a big part of that. She (Caroline) is always very done'

WHO WOULD WIN IN A FIGHT BETWEEN EDWARD CULLEN AND STEFAN SALVATORE?
'Stefan!'

Name:........ Candice Accola
Born:.......... 13 May 1987
From:......... Houston, Texas

At a very young age, Accola knew she wanted to be a performer. In her early teens, Accola found a California-based agent, moved to LA and soon had a deal for a CD titled *It's Always the Innocent Ones*. She finished high school via correspondence and graduated in 2005. Since then, Accola has been busy scoring parts in popular TV shows and films like *How I Met Your Mother*, *Hannah Montana & Miley Cyrus: Best of Both Worlds Concert* and *Hannah Montana: The Movie*.

STEVEN R McQUEEN
JEREMY GILBERT

Name:........ Terrence Steven McQueen II (screen name, Steven R McQueen)
Born:.......... 13 July 1988
From:......... Los Angeles, California

It would be safe to say that Steven R McQueen has acting in his blood. He is the grandson of actor Steve McQueen and the son of actor/producer Chad McQueen. His big acting break came in 2006, when he landed the role of Kyle Hunter in hit US show *Everwood*.

WHERE HAVE YOU SEEN HIM BEFORE?
Numbers, Without A Trace, CSI: Miami

ZACH ROERIG
MATT DONOVAN

Name:........ Zachary George Roerig
Born: .... 22 February 1985
From:......... Montpelier, Ohio

Zach was born in Montpelier, Ohio to Andrea and Daniel Roerig. He has a younger sister called Emily, and at high school he was a key member of the American football and wrestling teams. While he was growing up, Zach worked for his father and grandfather at Fackler Monuments, making gravestones. He made his television debut in 2004 in *Law & Order*, and has since appeared in shows like *As The World Turns* and *Friday Night Lights*.

MICHAEL TREVINO
TYLER LOCKWOOD

Name: Michael Trevino
Born: 25 January 1985
From: Montebello, California

Trevino was born and raised in California. He's landed roles in a string of hit US TV shows such as *Cold Case*, *Without A Trace*, *Charmed* and *90210*.

KAYLA EWELL
VICKI DONOVAN

Name: Kayla Noelle Ewell
Born: 27 August 1985
From: Long Beach, California

From a very early age, Ewell always loved everything to do with the stage. She studied dance, singing, and acting at the Orange County Song & Dance Company, and was spotted by a talent scout in 1999. Her first TV appearance was in *Freaks and Geeks*, and she went on to star in hit shows like *The Bold and the Beautiful*, *The O.C.*, *Veronica Mars* and *Entourage*.

THE CAST